NEITHER MAN NOR WOMAN IS SPELLED S.A.I.N.T.

SAMMY GOTT

Silkhaven Publishing, LLC

ISBN: 978-1-948997-29-4 (mobi)

ISBN: 978-1-948997-28-7 (epub)

ISBN: 978-1-948997-30-0 (paperback)

Library of Congress Control Number: 2019920487

Copyright (c) 2019, 2020, Sammy Lee Gott

(V1) – January 15, 2020

All rights reserved. No part of this book may be used or reproduced in any manner without the written permission of the author Sammy Lee Gott and the publisher Silkhaven Publishing, LLC with the exception in the case of brief quotations embodied in critical articles and reviews.

Printed in the United States of America.

Silkhaven Publishing, LLC does not have any control over and does not assume any responsibility for author or third–party Web sites or their content.

The scanning, uploading, and distribution of this book via the internet or via any other means without the permission of Silkhaven Publishing, LLC or Sammy Lee Gott is illegal and punishable by law. To obtain a copy of this novel, please purchase only through authorized electronic or print editions, and do not participate in or encourage electronic piracy of copyrighted materials.

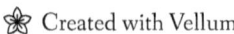 Created with Vellum

CONTENTS

Acknowledgments — v
My Perceptions — vii

Radical Feminism — 1
#MeToo Movement — 5
Women Use Sex to Get What They Want — 8
Dating — 11
Sex Before Marriage — 15
Abuse — 18
False Accusations — 22
Few men are sex fiends, deviates or pedophiles — 25
Masculinity Attitudes/Male Attitudes — 28
Why So Much Hate? — 32
Misogyny/Misandry — 34
What is a dysfunctional family? — 36
Media/Newspapers — 49
Do We Choose Love? — 54
Do U.S. Women Really Have it so Bad? — 55
What do men and women look for when dating? — 64
What is love about? — 67
A Love Story — 69
How Can We Change? — 73
Bring Back the Draft — 76
Press/Media — 78
What Can Women and Men Do? — 81
References/Background Resources — 85

Also by Sammy Gott — 95

ACKNOWLEDGMENTS

I want to thank all the writers, newspapers, magazines, books, and Google who I used for research. There is a listing of these sources in the back. Almost all of these articles and publishings happened in the years 2017-2019. Without an Internet, Smart News, Fox News and Flipboard, this book could not have happened. I also want to thank my friend William Boughton who gave me good advice and inspiration.

MY PERCEPTIONS

I have been watching with great concern today's women's movement. I feel empathy with what women are expressing but in some ways I feel betrayed and insulted by the way they are expressing their feelings.

Neither man nor woman is spelled **S A I N T,** but it seems that everytime one turns around, some woman or women's organization is demonizing a man or men and of course the news media churn this hatred.

Right up front I will tell you that my qualification to write this book is that I have lived through this man/woman dance for 77 years. I have watched civility between men and women almost disappear, with our interactions in many cases confrontational. I know what love is because I have loved my wife for forty-three years. I have three boys and one daughter that I adore. I want this book to help both sexes better understand each other.

My first drafts of this book were testy. But God sent me a friend who said this to me after editing the book, "Now I believe this can be a fine book but the book is quite angry, and appears to cast aspersions on all women, rather than some women whose behavior offends you."

I come from a dysfunctional family where both parents were alcoholics and my mother was an abusive parent (more on this later). I have been fighting misogyny all my life. About the time I think I have it whipped it raises its ugly head. I realized that I was not fair to all the kind, considerate and loving women out there. This feminist movement in my opinion has gone from trying to help women to showing them how to hate men. My writings in my first tries, as a man, was like a mirror to the radical feminist movement and showed too much hatred. I scrapped those first books and started over with this one.

I want to write a book about the love that men and women have for each other that is being poisoned by this out of control feminist movement.

A new heart also will I give you, and a new spirit will I put within you: and I will take away the stony heart out of your flesh, and I will give you a heart of flesh.
Ezekiel 36:26 KJV

RADICAL FEMINISM

Feminism- is something I have been trying to understand all my life. Here is a quote that Pat Robertson made in the 90's:

> "The feminist agenda is not about equal rights for women. It is about a socialist, anti-family political movement that encourages women to leave their husbands, kill their children, practice witchcraft, destroy capitalism, and become lesbians."

Mr. Robertson's definition is something I can't agree with, and I try to avoid in my continuing attempts to understand feminism, but one wonders what caused this statement.

Marriage- this quote from *LIFESIT Jan. 2013 is scary:*

> "Young men giving up on marriage: Women aren't women anymore" (42A).

Susanne Venker's article *"The War on Men"* states that one of the major reasons that men are giving up on marriage is

"men are tired of being told there's something fundamentally wrong with them. Tired of being told that if women aren't happy, it's men's fault."

When Venker, in her research, asked men why they would never get married, the answer was:

"women aren't women anymore. Feminism, which teaches women to think of men as the enemy, has made women **angry** and **defensive,** though often unknowingly."

Is Equality Ruining Your Marriage?

Fox News, Sept. 2017, by Suzanne Venker (74A): New research at the University of Illinois examined data on nearly 1,500 men and 1,800 women between the ages of 52 and 60 found that couples who resist traditional gender roles, or who shoot for a so-called equal marriage, are less happy than those who swim with the tide of tradition.

Women and Gender studies

Check universities today and you might find a course called "Women and Gender Studies." When you go on line to check these courses out you will probably find some reference to the LGBTQ movement.

In my opinion, after sitting in one of these classes many years ago, some of these courses teach the superiority of women and that men are the root of most of life's problems. Participants in some cases get extra credit to publicly demonstrate against female suppression and toxic masculinity. Women who go through these courses end up in all phases of our lives spouting the propaganda they learned from these courses.

One of the biggest problems I see, with the hatred towards men, is that women who do not believe that men are the root of all evils, will not speak up. Do the bullies in the feminist movements intimidate them? This hatred of men is not going to stop until women stop it.

Why Are So Many Campus Feminists Anti-Male?

This article written May 7, 2018, by Warren Farrell(23), is six pages in length, and has so much to say. I recommend everyone who is interested in solving some of these man/woman problems read it. I want to just include here some quotes from that article for everyone to think about:

> "It was then – in the early seventies – that I began to experience that campus feminists wanted men to understand women but had no interest in understanding men."

Does the solution include an evolutionary shift in the male-female tango? Yes. But let's do it with respect for women. When females are encouraged to speak up and males are told to shut up, that does not generate respect for women.

> "And let's do it without undermining feminist progress toward female equality. When both sexes get drunk and have

consensual sex, if the drinking erases her accountability, but not his, that undermines the responsibilities that accompany equality. When due process is eliminated to protect only women, that also undermines the responsibilities that accompany equality."

"In aggregate, advancing a narrative of victim power ultimately leaves girls and women protected, but powerless. Yes, the over-protected are more loved; but the over-protected are less respected. The next evolutionary step we need in the male-female tango is equal accountability, equal respect, equal listening to both sexes, and equally loving both sexes."

Anti-male activities in colleges take many avenues, the first being enrollments. The University of Minnesota (14) has recently changed their rules on two scholarships because of an anti-male allegation concerning women-only scholarships.

#METOO MOVEMENT

From Wikipedia, the free encyclopedia

THE **METOO MOVEMENT** (OR **#METOO MOVEMENT**), WITH ITS many local and international equivalents, is a movement against sexual harassment and sexual assault.

#MeToo spread virally in October 2017 as a hash tag used on social media in an attempt to demonstrate the widespread prevalence of sexual assault and harassment, especially in the workplace.

It followed soon after the sexual misconduct allegations against Harvey Weinstein. Tarana Burke, an American social activist and community organizer, began using the phrase "Me Too" as early as 2006, and the phrase was later popularized by American actress Alyssa Milano(11), on Twitter in 2017. Milano encouraged victims of sexual harassment to tweet about it and "give people a sense of the magnitude of the problem." This was met with success that included but was not limited to high-profile posts from several American celebrities, including Gwyneth Paltrow, Ashley Judd, Jennifer Lawrence, and Uma Thurman.

Asia Argento

From Wikipedia, the free encyclopedia

> **Asia Argento** (Italian: [aːzja ar dʒɛnto]; born **Aria Maria Vittoria Rossa Argento**, 20 September 1975) is an Italian actress, director, singer and model. The daughter of filmmaker Dario Argento, she is best known for her roles in the films XXX (2002), Land of the Dead (2005) and Marie Antoinette (2006). Awards she has won include two David di Donatello for Best Actress for Let's not Keep in Touch (1994) and Traveling Companion (1996).

After the Weinstein scandal in 2017, she became a leader of the "#MeToo" women's rights movement. In August 2018, *The New York Times* detailed allegations that Argento sexually assaulted actor Jimmy Bennett(21 &25) in 2013 when he was 17 and she was 37; Argento denied the allegations but she agreed to pay $380,000 to the actor who accused her.

Is it not amazing that one of the beginning leaders of the #MeToo movement was accused of raping an underage young boy (5)? Women do not believe that they can rape a man because all men want sex. A good example of this is Stephanie Peterson, a teacher who taught at New Smyrna Beach Middle School. She had sex with a 14-year-old student. Her defense lawyers said, "She should serve less than the minimum sentence for the crime because the boy was a willing participant."(57)

I wonder if one could dig up nasty little things on others in the movement? At least someone in the movement knows how it feels to be falsely (she said) accused and all that goes with it.

Tammy Bruce (4) wrote an outstanding article, *The Democrats "believe all women" fraud*, published November 11, 2018 on

Foxnews.com. Everyone was ordered to dump due process and "believe all women."

Now we are seeing in an article written by Christal Hayes in USA Today on Nov. 2, 2018 that some of these accusers are being referred to the Department of Justice for prosecution because of their outright lies during the Brett Kavanaugh confirmation hearings (36a).

Pamela Anderson said it all in a Foxnews.com article written by Tyler McCarthy (47) November 05, 2018,

---

"Feminism can go too far. I'm a feminist, but I think that this third wave of feminism is a bore. I think it paralyzes men."

WOMEN USE SEX TO GET WHAT THEY WANT

Is it not amusing that women use sex to get power, position and possessions and then get upset because men use power, position and possessions to get sex?

Women have always played men with sex to get what they want for as long as men and women have been on earth. All one has to do is read history starting with the Bible to know this is true.

So let's stop the nonsense and tell the truth. Without sex there would be no children or future for mankind. Without the sex drive of men and women the world as we know it would not exist. Women play their games to get what they want and men play their games to get sex.

The big reason that we have outlawed prostitution in this country is not because it is immoral, but because prostitution interferes with what women who are not prostitutes can get for their charms.

Reporter's affair with Senate official

Howard Kurtz (42) wrote an article for FoxNews.com June 27, 2018 concerning a female reporter, Ali Watkins, who worked for a number of news organizations, finally working her way up to a position on the New York Times by using her three-year affair with a Senate intelligence committee official, James Wolfe, by getting information from him and then writing articles.

In most cases the news organizations knew the information was coming from the sleeping arrangement. After Watkins and Wolfe split, she started dating someone else on the committee. The Times then wrote:

"The relationship has prompted concern in many newsrooms that Ms. Watkins' conduct has made journalists, and particularly women, vulnerable to unfounded accusations of exchanging sex for information."

What? Unfounded?

There are many things done in this country to accommodate women

Go to many states in the United States and one will find laws written for the protection of women only. Next time you read of a man being accused by a woman of sexual misconduct and her name does not appear but his is in the headlines, her name is likely being protected by one of those laws.

A man can be forced into parenthood against his will or have his child aborted against his will, even though the child has 50/50 genetics. Laws have been changed or enacted because women believe that "it's my body."

Job quotas exist purely for women, without taking into account any other variables. I can remember forty years ago when this *poor woman* attitude started in the work place, I was ordered by the company to hire women, even if they were not qualified for the job. Most of them used the company's time and resources and did not stay.

I read an interesting article today that really set my mind to thinking about how this country accommodates women.

The article was written by Dennis Prager in TownHall on April 09, 2019. Yes, he is a man and it is written from a man's point of view. The article is **Are Women Malcontents?**

Why do I find this article so fascinating? Because, one hears his thoughts on men's thinking these days. Mr. Prager talks about the book *The Feminine Mystique, by Betty Friedan,* written 56 years ago and all the complaints that were brought up in the book. Mr. Prager said this:

> "In the 56 years since 'The Feminine Mystique' was published, every complaint Friedan made regarding the situation of the American woman has been addressed. Yet, if you were to listen to many American women today, you would think nothing has improved. Every women's group and millions of individual women say women are 'oppressed' despite the fact that virtually nothing remains of the 'feminine mystique' described by Friedan."

DATING

As a teenager starting to date, I thought that girls wanted to date me because of who I was. Boys find out that a good portion of the time, girls want to date them because they drive a nice car, are sports stars, can get them in other circles having power in the politics of the school, and cost-free entertainment. This cost-free entertainment for girls/women is a driving factor in dating for some women. I have heard many girls/women say that if the male did not pay for it, they would not date them.

As a chauffeur, I have heard women in the back seat talking about playing men so they can have a good time at the expense of the male. No wonder some men think that women are selling their bodies.

I could see in a past era, when most women did not work, why men would pay their way. Many women now work and sometimes get paid more than men. There is no reason why women cannot pay their way unless they are trying to use the males. Men are not stupid. Men know when they are being used; thus, the attitude that the woman owes the man something back in return. If the women want a situation of respect, then they need to pay their own way.

I just read an article in Fox News by Edmund DeMarche (15) titled, *"Dine-and-dash dater" faces 10 felony counts for allegedly skipping out on dates before bill* (40). It seems that this young man would go out on dates with women and then get up and leave before the bill showed up. Of course most of the women had to pay the bill and this upset them no *end*. He was charged and pleaded no contest to three misdemeanor counts of defrauding an innkeeper by nonpayment and one misdemeanor count of petty theft. He was sentenced to 120 days in county jail and three years probation.

My first thought is how did the restaurants know that he was the one who was supposed to pay the bill? They assumed and/or were told by the woman that the man was supposed to pay. Does this mean that all the women who would not pay the bill should be in jail?

As males we are taught by women to be bold and ask for the date. Just ask women, a good majority of them will tell you that they expect the male to ask them out, make the first move to put his arm around her, initiate the first kiss, ask her to be engaged and so on. Nowadays, all the years of training by women that we should be bold is wrong.

Don't dare ask a woman out on a date using words they do not like. Don't make hints that you like them or you want to date them because now it is sexual harassment. Men are beginning to think everything is sexual harassment for women, unless the woman initiates it and then it might be if they don't like the way it turns out.

I cannot tell you how many times in my life I have been sexually harassed by women (using today's definition of sexual harassment) as they show me their breasts, thighs or their private parts, or they touch me on my thighs, back, arms and butt. I have on a few occasions had them grab my testicles. I can't count the many times that a woman has made suggestive remarks to me. But because they did it, there was no sexual harassment. If you are a woman reading this book stop and think about how many times you have done the above things. Did the males say anything? They should have.

November 5, 2018, Laura Fitzpatrick(24) wrote an article for The Telegraph where she described a situation where a male teacher accused a female teacher of sexual assault. It seems at a teacher/parent meeting, the female teacher ripped open the man's shirt and sexually assaulted him by grabbing his testicles. The female teacher admitted she did it. The prosecution decided not to prosecute. I can guarantee that if the tables were turned, the man would go to jail.

Dating at any age is a terrifying experience for a man. What can a man expect on a date in this day and age? Can he act like a man or is his masculinity toxic?

Dating is a precursor to marriage. The Pew Research Center recently found that the number of women ages 18-34 saying that having a successful marriage is one of the most important things rose from 28 percent to 37 percent since 1997. The number of young adult men saying the same thing dropped from 35 percent to 29 percent in the same time period. Let's think about this. Susanne Venker's Article(83), "The War on Men" states that "men are tired of being told there's something fundamentally wrong with them. Tired of being told that if women aren't happy, it's men's fault."

Dating has gotten to be quite a chore for men. It seems that nothing they do is right with women. I believe that this joke has a lot that we need to think about:

> Jane comes home from a blind date. When she walks through the door her roommate Alice notices something is wrong. Jane goes immediately to her bedroom and Alice follows her. Jane proceeds to take off her wig and put it on a styrofoam head, takes her eyelashes off and puts them in a plastic container, takes her padded bra and girdle off

and puts them in a drawer, slips out of her support panty hose and puts them away. Then she goes into the bathroom and begins to take off the many layers of makeup. About this time, Alice asks, "What is the matter?" Jane then says, "You know, there are not any real men around nowadays."

SEX BEFORE MARRIAGE

It used to be that sex came after marriage. Now, oftentimes, it comes before marriage. If the dating partners choose to wait, that solves a lot of problems.

Men have a very strong sex drive. I am not about to pretend I know why God did this, but as a male, I do know the strength of that drive. The strength of males' sex drive is so strong that they have to work each day to keep it under control. I also know that males are very visual and audial. Our sex drive is controlled by the views of women and the words they use with us.

Here are a few problems that I see in this man and woman relationship dance:

- *Since we men are highly visual, what you wear does make a difference. Women can- not tease us by showing us your breasts, thighs, bare back and other bare parts and expect us not to be aroused.*
- *Women cannot get drunk with a man and expect a man's drunken mind to be a gentleman.*
- *Women cannot go out on the town having drinks, dinner*

and entertainment and have a man pay the whole bill and then be surprised if the man expects something in return.
- If you want a man to notice your mind and other capabilities don't emphasize your body.
- You cannot use your body to get what you want, and complain that the man did not act properly.
- There are only two words that can be used in a sensual situation and they are **yes** and **no**. Yes means you are not a victim. A no means the person saying no has the obligation to leave the encounter if physically possible. One can't say yes and still be a victim even if the encounter did not go the way one imagined.
- Both men and women should be very careful with what they say about any encounter with the opposite sex. Always remember the reputation of either is very fragile. Once lost it is hard to get back.

It seems to this man there are too many women making accusations about their male partners that cause legal problems and ruining of their reputations without having to prove it. Don't get me wrong; if a man sexually assaults or abuses a woman he must suffer the consequences. But I believe it must be proven.

I hear of too many cases nowadays where a woman will make an accusation using the man's full name while often the law protects her name from being used. Without a process of law and proof, the man's reputation is ruined, and then the accusation is proven false. The damage to the man has already been done. It seems the accusation appears on the front page of the newspaper but the retraction appears on page twenty.

Is this what pre-marital sex will look like in the future?(61)

There is a new app called **LegalFling** https://legalfling.io/ that claims to have your back when it comes to engaging in sex, by giving one legal consent when used.

Created by a Dutch Company, LegalFling, the app "allows you to request consent from any of your contacts." It will send your request for sex along with your "sexual preferences." The app will enter the consenting participants into a binding legal contract.

Can you imagine entering into a legal contract while dating to protect yourself from legal action if you have sex? Run, do not walk, to the nearest exit!

ABUSE

This is a subject I have had some experience with. No, I have never, and will never abuse my wife or children. One of my parents, my mother, was an abuser. She physically, verbally and mentally abused my father and all of us four boys.

The abuse was such that everyone carried the burden of that parent's action on their shoulders all their life. My oldest brother ran away from home at age fifteen and joined the military. My older twin brothers and I joined the military the day after we turned seventeen just to get out of the house. It was easier to go to war (Vietnam War) then stay home and continue to be abused.

I can remember many a night when my mother threw things, tried to cut, or shoot at my father. To this day I can remember the beatings that I received from her.

According to *The National Domestic Violence Hotline*(38) *www.thehotline.org:*

"More than 1 in 3 women (35.6%) and more than 1 in 4 men (28.5%) in the United States have experienced rape, physical violence and/or stalking by an intimate partner in their lifetime."

Mark Brooks, chairman of the Mankind Initiative:

" I believe this number would be greater for men if they weren't too ashamed to admit to anyone that they were being raped, abused or stalked by their female partner."

The National Domestic Violence Hotline also states:

"Nearly half of all women and men in the United States have experienced psychological aggression by an intimate partner in their lifetime (48.4 and 48.8, respectively)(53)."

An article in **The Follow**: by Charles Hymas(39) and Patrick Scott, November 2018 had some interesting statistics of domestic abuse in England from **The Office for National Statistics (ONS)**.

1. Male victims reporting domestic abuse increased from 10.4% in 2014-2015 to 14.7% in 2018.
2. Male victims of abuse attributed the increase to men's willingness to talk about their suffering. More men are finding the courage to go to the police. "The police have thankfully also moved a long way from the stereotypical

> view of domestic abuse that it was only a crime affecting women. They are far more inclusive in their approach".
3. One charity stated, "A third of domestic violence victims are male yet only 0.8% refuge beds are reserved for them."
4. Steve Allan, Trustee and Secretary of Men's Aid, said: "Generally speaking, abuse directed against men is getting more noticed but there is still a bias against men. When you see a stock image depicting domestic violence, it's always of a woman cowering from a man."

It is important for all of us to remember, no matter female or male, psychological aggression, physical abuse and rape happen to both sexes by the opposite sex, or the same sex. Let's quit trying to demonize the men and find ways to stop this bad behavior by both sexes.

Not enough is said about mental and psychological abuse. Believe me when I say that mental and psychological abuse may not leave marks on the body but it leaves marks on the soul.

Woman realizes that she's been accidentally abusing her husband this whole time

Website **https:www.hrtwarming.com/woman-realizes-that-shes-been-accidentally -** If I could accomplish anything with this book, I would want it to be getting women to read **Mary Sue's(69)** article in **Hart Warming** dated May 18, 2015. One can get it by going to the following:

> ***abusing-her-husband-this-whole-time-wow/***

I read the article and I took it to my wife and told her it was important to me that she read it. After she read it we talked about how a lot of women we know verbally abuse their husbands and don't realize they are doing it. **Please read this article.**

FALSE ACCUSATIONS

FALSE ACCUSATIONS HAVE BEEN GOING ON SINCE THE BEGINNING of time. I only started paying attention to them in the 1980's when Al Sharpton got famous with the Tawana Brawley (56) Case. This young woman claimed that four white men had raped her in the woods, in Wappinger's Falls, New York. A Grand Jury found the allegations were an elaborate hoax.

Published in foxnews.com March 02, 2018(65):

A Clemson student had been arrested after deputies say she falsely accused a man of raping her at a fraternity house party. "As the investigation continued and evidence was gathered in the case and based upon that evidence, it was determined that the sexual relations between the female and male at the Fraternity House were consensual and that the female had not been truthful in the information that she provided to the investigator in the case." The male student is considering legal action against the police and the college.

Michigan woman who lied about being raped on college campus sentenced to 45 days in jail.

Body cam footage contradicts woman's claim trooper sexually assaulted her; her lawyer apologizes. (64)

Charges dropped against Florida college students accused of gang rape.

Woman accused a male police officer of raping her on the side of the road after her arrest for shoplifting. A female officer did the entire pat downs and body cam proved nothing happened. Also car camera proved no stops made from point of arrest to the jail.

Rapper Drake files lawsuit against woman who attempted to get money from him claiming he got her pregnant. (34)

School pays male student $47,000 after it punished him based on no more than an accusation. (66)

Woman accused of lying about being raped offered plea deal. (1)

These false accusations happen too often. I think the only way to stop them is if the accusations are proven to be false, have the accuser serve the same sentence the accused would have had to serve. Check out the sentence of 45 days in jail for the woman who made a false accusation of rape. Now, if convicted, the man would have spent years in jail.

The Judge Kavanaugh fiasco was a terrible example of just how unproved accusations are being used in the political world.

After almost ruining Judge Kavanaugh's life and career, not one shred of evidence was produced to prove any of the accusations. Charges have been filed on many of the accusers (36a).

I hope that the justice system is used to show that false accusations can be costly to the accuser. The process has been started to charge two women of the group of accusers with lying to congress (36a).

FEW MEN ARE SEX FIENDS, DEVIATES OR PEDOPHILES

IF YOU TRY AND KEEP UP WITH THE NEWS YOU WILL BE bombarded with newspaper or TV news stories that project that men are sex fiends, sex deviates or pedophiles. Yet one very seldom hears about women sex fiends, sex deviates or pedophiles. I wonder why that is? (Possibly because there are fewer of them?)

Back in the 80's I used to work out with an older man who was a fine gentleman. He told me that in his neighborhood he used to take long walks in the afternoon. When he came across children in the yard he would always give them candy, which he carried with him. With tears in his eyes he said that his wife had asked him not to do that anymore because she feared someone would accuse him of being a pedophile.

I couldn't believe that could happen. Fast forward forty years later, one day driving as a chauffeur, I had to pick a client up at a big office complex. The complex had a very large parking lot and the temperature was close to 100 degrees. You can imagine how hot that concrete was. I drove to the far end where there was a large oak tree that provided some shade. I parked in the shade while I waited and kept the car running so that the air conditioner would work.

Across the road about fifty yards I noticed a school bus parked. The woman driver was acting strangely, waving her fist and yelling about something. I thought her actions were strange but did not give them much thought.

When it came time to pick up the client I pulled in front of the office building, parked and texted him that I was out front. Before the client came out the security people came up to me and asked me what I was doing there. I explained to them that I was a chauffeur working for a limousine service here to pick up a client.

It seems because my car was parked under the shade tree facing a building that I did not even know was a school, the female school bus driver called security and told them a suspected pervert was parked in front of the school trying to pick up a child.

At first thought one could not fault her for being so concerned for the children's safety, but on second thought, she would never have called if it had been a woman in the same car. Because I was a man, danger was afoot.

In my research fewer than five percent of males in the USA are pedophiles. There is no indication that woman pedophiles do not exist at the same rate, nor that they do, either. There are no reliable statistics, except to say that they do exist.

Just in 2018 these stories came out in print:

- *Woman Arrested After Posting a Video of Herself Raping 5-year-old boy.* (3)
- *Female Primary school head admits child sex offenses as outraged parents thought she was "off sick."* (74)
- *A Chicago Public School teaching assistant is facing*

accusations that she sexually assaulted a young student at least twice nearly a decade ago.(37)
- Ex-Plano teacher who sent nude pictures, played beer pong with student gets probation for improper relationship. (8)
- Male student molested by female teacher awarded $2.1M.(7)
- Teacher called "Kim Kardashian" by students pleads guilty to sex acts with boys. (63)
- Female staff member admits to having sex with five male teenage students at a prestigious school – but says she only did it because she was blackmailed. (80)
- Woman arrested and charged for sending X-rated pictures to a 15 year-old that she taught. This woman was under the age of 30 and had won a state beauty contest in the past. She could have dated any man but she chose a 15 year-old. (13)
- Substitute teacher, 23, accused of having sex with two students, including 14-year-old. (28)
- Teen's dad busted Texas teacher, 44, having sex with student in car, police say. (29)
- Special Ed teacher, mother of 5 gets 10 years for sex with teen boy student. (30)
- Married English teacher, 32, pleads not guilty to charge of booze-filled sex with teen boy student. (31)

I had security called on me because I was parked outside a school. Maybe security people should have been in the school.

MASCULINITY ATTITUDES/MALE ATTITUDES

If one would go to https://metoomvmt.org, you can see a number of **Statistics on Masculinity attitudes/Male Attitudes;** some of these are listed below (read further why these statistics are flawed):

31.7% percent of college men would have sexual intercourse with a woman against her will "if nobody would ever know and there wouldn't be any consequences."(19) Only 13.6 percent of these men said they would have "any intentions to rape a woman" in the same situation.

The above information came from a paper written in December 2014 by three women, Sarah R. Edwards, Kathryn A Bradshaw and Verlin B. Hinsz(20) in a paper called "Denying Rape but Endorsing forceful intercourse: Exploring Differences Among Responders."

On face value some would say this is shocking. Men are devils.

But this paper is just another piece of information where the study was manipulated to get the results that were wanted.

Robby Soave of Reason wrote an article (Would a Third of Males Students Commit Rape? – Methodological Flaws in New Study) rebutting the facts stated. (79).

Here is his reasoning:

1. *The study considered the statement of only 73 men out of 10+ million undergraduate students in the United States. The data is flawed to extrapolate this to a larger body.*
2. *All the students surveyed came from the same school with no replication, which also complicated the issue.*
3. *The students were given extra credit to take part in the survey. Students who need extra credit to pass may be suffering from various issues be they mental health, physical well-being, sports related, etc.*
4. *How many people would break any law if they knew they could get away with it, man or woman.*
5. *Saying one would do something bad if there are no consequences is not the same as doing those bad things.*

50% of men ages 18 to 34 agree with this statement: "If your partner is willing to kiss you she must be willing to do other sexual acts."

What a loaded question. This proves that men are demons. Maybe these men have had sexual relations with women and their experience makes the statement true.

One in three women have been a victim of either an attempted or completed rape in her lifetime.

Based the National Crime Victimization Survey (NCVS) from 2015 to 2016, the rate of rape or sexual assault declined from 1.6 to 1.1 victimizations per 1,000 persons age 12 or older, and from 2.7 to 1.8 among females age 12 or older.

According to the NCVS the number of rapes in the country went from 431,840 in 2015 to 298,410 in 2016. For 2016, the Federal Bureau of Investigation's (FBI) Uniform Crime Reporting (UCR) program reported .4 rapes per 1000 residents.

If one were to believe the #MeToo movement our country is being overrun with rapists. The facts say differently. There are way too many people writing articles on this subject using information from surveys that are set up to manipulate the numbers to fit their narrative.

December 3, 2018, Gillian Tan and Katia Porsecanski (70) wrote an article in Bloomberg Business on a new Wall Street rule called the "Pence Effect." Men in order to protect themselves from unreasonable political correctness are staying away from women executives. Many male executives in many different companies will not have dinners, will not sit next to them on flights, avoid one-on-one meetings and if they stay in the same hotel on a business trip will book their room on a different floor.

Unless men start seeing some fairness in this #MeToo movement, one will see the "Pence Effect" spread.

I believe there is too much hate between the sexes being taught and not enough how do we live together and love each other.

There is a class-action lawsuit pending in Rhode Island suing the state, the governor, and education officials, because the state fails to prepare their students to fully participate in civic life. I believe that there ought to be lawsuits across this country suing the states because they do not teach young girls and boys how to get along with one another.

I also believe that one of our biggest problems with children not being taught how to get along with one another is that we have many dysfunctional families in this country that cannot teach their children how to get along with other people because the parents do not know how to get along themselves. More on this later.

WHY SO MUCH HATE?

TEN BENEFITS OF CONFLICT

Conflict is not always bad for human beings. An article In Entrepreneur by Sherie Campbell, July 2016, "The 10 Benefits of Conflict"(4A) points out some of the advantages of conflict:

1. Opens our eyes to new ideas
2. Opportunity to verbalize needs
3. Teaches flexibility
4. Teaches us to listen
5. Teaches us patterns of behavior
6. Leads to solutions
7. Practice communications skills
8. Helps us to set limits
9. Practice emotional control
10. Allows us to differentiate ourselves

We can see that a lot of things get done when we humans have conflict. Conflict also can cause stress and worry. (35A) If we are under stress and worry too long, our body produces hormones that can make us ill. How we handle this continuous stress can affect our moods, attitudes and even our lifespan. Stress over a long period of time does change your brain.

MISOGYNY/MISANDRY

MISOGYNY IS THE DISLIKE OF, CONTEMPT FOR, OR INGRAINED prejudice against women or girls.

Misandry is the dislike of, contempt for, or ingrained prejudice against men or boys.

In my section **My Perceptions** one can see that there is misandry from the females in a lot of the articles and misogyny in a lot of my statements about the articles.

So let's be honest with each other—the dislike, contempt and prejudice is on both sides. We must understand the root causes of this hatred in order to make changes.

In the preceding pages I point out many flaws in women but I want to say that women have a lot of legitimate reasons to complain about their treatment from men. We are all human, and the flaws in the human race are equal on both sexes.

Causes of Misogyny or Misandry?

- *Social exclusions*
- *Sex discrimination*
- *Hostility*
- *Patriarchy*
- *Matriarchy*
- *Male/Female Privilege*
- *Belittling opposite sex*
- *Disenfranchisement of Men or Women*
- *Violence against opposite sex*
- *Sexual objectification*
- *Dysfunctional Families*

Some Major Causes of Dysfunctional Families

I believe the root cause for many of our problems in the U.S. (and perhaps the world) comes from people growing up in dysfunctional families.

I can speak to this subject with a good amount of knowledge because I was raised in an abusive dysfunctional family.

One never outgrows the trauma of it.

One just tries to adjust one's life. My brothers and I, even though we are all in our seventies and eighties, carry the mental and physical scars of that upbringing even today.

It is said that the traits of a dysfunctional family pass down four generations. I have worked very hard to make sure that was not true in my family, but I must admit due to my mother being the abusing parent, even today I find misogyny creeps into my thoughts and life.

If you are interested in what it takes to survive a dysfunctional family, read my book "*When Love Doesn't Start at Home.*"

WHAT IS A DYSFUNCTIONAL FAMILY?

CATHERINE HUANG WROTE AN ARTICLE *8 COMMON Characteristics of a Dysfunctional Family*38A that listed the following characteristics:

1. **Addiction-***The addiction can be drugs, alcohol, or a combination of both.*
2. **Perfectionism-***When perfectionism is highly regarded and parents place unrealistic expectations on their kids to succeed, the children may grow up with self-image and self-esteem issues, believing that they will never be good enough.*
3. **Abuse-***Abuse can occur between two spouses, from a parent to a child, or between two sibling children.*
4. **Unpredictability and Fear**—*They are patterns often produced from abuse, but can also exist from a parent's or spouse's financial handling or emotional and reactive behavior.*
5. **Conditional Love**—*When conditional love is*

exercised, it can make family members feel used or cheated.
6. **Lack of Boundaries**—A lack of boundaries often occurs when one parent tries to be controlling and dominant through anger.
7. **Lack of Intimacy**—It's important for family members to provide the choice of being with one another because they want to, not because they have to.
8. **Poor Communication**—When family members can't express themselves due to strained or nonexistent communication, they may end up feeling unheard, invisible, or misunderstood.

Pew Research Center Facts on the American Family 2015 (58B)

In 1960 there was one dominant family form. At that time 73% of all children were living in a family with two married parents in their first marriage. By 2015 that number had dropped to less than half (46%).

In 2014 one government study found that over a three-year period, about three-in-ten (31%) children younger than 6 had experienced a major change in their family or household structure, in the form of parental divorce, separation, marriage, cohabitation or death.

Black children and those with less educated parents are less likely to be living in two-parent households.

The living arrangements of black children stand in stark contrast to the other major racial and ethnic groups. The majority —54%—are living with a single parent.

Non-marital births continued to rise until mid-2000s, when the share of births to unmarried women stabilized at around 40%.

Among Black women, 71% of births are now outside of marriage, as are about 53% of births to Hispanic women. In contrast, 29% of births to white women occur outside of marriage.

About one-in-five children born within a marriage will experience the breakup of that marriage by age 9.

Family life has been greatly affected by the movement of more and more mothers into the workforce. In 1975, less than half of mothers (47%) with children younger than 18, were in the labor force. Labor force participation today stands at 70% among all mothers of children younger than 18.

While Googling dysfunctional families, I came across an article called **The Big Answer—Family Dysfunction. (72A)** This article had many jewels of wisdom. Below are just a few of them:

1. *John Bradshaw, a family-systems therapy advocate and family dynamics expert, cites research that found 96 percent of all families to be, to some degree "dysfunctional," that is, the system by which the family interacts is distorted by the addictions and compulsions of*

one or more members and, so, ignores the needs of each individual.
2. *As 96 percent of all families are to some degree emotionally impaired, the unhealthy rules we're living by are handed down from one generation to another and ultimately to society at large. Our society is sick because our families are sick.*
3. *There's a sharp rise in the proportion of adolescents getting psychiatric counseling, most of which is attributable to children in one-parent homes.*
4. *The inability of the family to carry out its basic functions, particularly the socialization of children and the passing on of a culture and character and competence to the next generation. This was once accomplished in the family; it is now being accomplished by other institutions.*

Additional causes of a dysfunctional family

Only one parent raising the children (33A)

- Out of all the single mothers, 45% of them were never married.
- Only 60% of single mothers are employed on a full time basis.
- Twenty-four million children, 1 out of 3, live without their biological father in the home.
- 63% of child suicides occur from homes that do not have a father.
- 90% of children who choose to run away or become homeless come from homes that do not have a father.

- Kids who grow up in a home with a single mother only are 20 times more likely to end up in prison.

All these scary statistics come from an article written by Brandon Gaille May 24, 2017. (33A)

All the above prove how very important it is for both the father and mother to live in the home and be active in their children's lives.

Government Discourages Marriage

Sheila Weber in her Feb. 11, 2018 article in Fox News article (78A) said:

> "Marriage is one of the most effective anti-poverty programs around. But far too often, government assistance programs for people of low income discourage marriage, because tying the knot reduces government welfare assistance payments."

According to the Heritage Foundation, when parents are married the probability of a child living in poverty drops by an amazing amount – 82 percent.

Growing up in a family in poverty puts a lot of unnecessary stress on the children and the parents. Helping the American family financially should take priority over many other things that the government spends money on.

In fact, I think it would be nice to give a sizable monetary bonus to people who get married. It would probably save the government money spent in welfare payments.

. . .

Low Wages

Have you wondered why 70% of mothers in the USA have to work? I am sure that a good portion of these mothers want to work but I think a majority of them would rather stay at home and be with their children.

According to Google, the average family has 1.8 children. A family that has a husband and wife with 1.8 children would be 3.8 individuals. The average cost of living in the USA per individual today is $12,863.00 per year. Multiply $12,863 by 3.8 and it gives you an average annual cost of living for this family of $48,879. Now compare that to the average male salary between ages 25 – 34 of $41,951. One can quickly see why so many mothers have to get a job. Now we have no parent at home with the children for a substantial part of the day.

I believe corporations are the biggest villains in the USA for the poor pay of the average worker.

The people who do all the work are the people that make the least in a corporation.

Let's look at one new corporation that has been in the headlines recently, UBER. UBER was started March of 2009. Its estimated worth as of August 2018 was 76 billion dollars. In about ten years from its beginning, it has grown to a $76 billion company.

Where do you think most of this worth came from? **The drivers**!

According to an article by Eric Reed written Dec. 11, 2018 in *The Street Vidio (60A)*, UBER drivers make an average of $36,525 annually. They have to pay their expenses of doing business plus

FICA contributions, health insurance, retirement contributions, and personal liability insurance. One can only imagine how little their take-home pay is.

In my opinion, corporations under-pay their workers for the work they do while the officers and the stockholders suck out most of the profits.

Corporations make up 5% of businesses but earn 62% of revenues in the USA. US Corporations market cap in US dollars:

Apple Inc. $465.91 Billion
Exxon Mobile Corporation $420.79 Billion
Google Inc. $409.98 Billion
Microsoft Corporation $311.61 Billion
Berkshire Hathaway $281.36 Billion
Johnson & Johnson $257.74 Billion
General Electric Company $255.67 Billion

One wonders what pocket all this wealth came out of? I believe it was all the underpaid employees that worked for these companies.

Of course, the CEO's of these corporations along with senior officers are not hurting for pay. *According to Forbes, average CEO pay in 2018 was 361 times more than the average worker in his or her company was paid.*

David M. Zaslav, the president and chief executive officer of media company *Discover, Inc.*, came in at No. 1 of all corporate CEO's with compensation of $129.4 million per year, according to the Wall Street Journal.

There is no way you can convince me that anyone should be paid that much.

A recent article by BARRONS titled "Americans Don't Save for Retirement Because They Don't Earn Enough Money" stated:

> "Too few Americans are saving for retirement. Those who do save are putting away too little. It is only a matter of time before this sparks an economic and political crisis"(1b).

This problem goes to most of the profits of corporations going to shareholders, officers or growth and the employees being underpaid.

The Federal Reserve reports that as of 2017, 41% of American households could not easily cover a $400.00 emergency expense. (1A)

In my youth I worked in employee benefit programs; I would design and implement various benefit programs.

At that time there were a lot of "Defined Benefit Pension Plans." As of 2016, only 30% of American households had access to a defined-benefit plan and only 52% participated in a defined-contribution plan (like a 401K).

The US Government allowed companies to raid the reserves of the defined-benefit plans, close them down and replace them with 401K thrift plans.

The difference is that under the defined benefit plan one could retire with a good percentage of their top ten years annual wage as a pension (most of the money for a Defined Benefit Pension Plan is contributed by the employer)

Under the 401k plans, the biggest portion of contributions are by the employee—an employee who does not make enough to contribute or to send his children through college.

The above article (1A) came up with a comprehensive solution to the retirement crisis:

- *Ensure that every worker earns sufficient income to be able to save.*
- *Broaden participation in defined-contribution savings plans by making them available to everyone and auto-enrolling.*
- *Secure and enhance Social Security to ensure a minimum income for all seniors.*

Will any of the above get done? Probably not; all the answers require employers to put more money into the pot.

Coming from a dysfunctional family I can attest to lack of money being a major cause for the problems in the family.

My father retired from the US Air Force as a Master Sergeant. He and my mother only had a sixth grade education. I watched them not make enough money to support their family. We lived in poverty as they tried to raise four children.

High Cost of Borrowing Money

So we have good portion of this country's workers being under-paid and the banks come along and take advantage of them by charging too much to borrow money. Here is a list of the largest ten banks in the USA by total assets:

JPMorgan Chase & Co. $2.62 Trillion
Bank of America Corp. $2.34 Trillion
Citigroup Inc. $1.93 Trillion
Wells Fargo & Co. $1.87 Trillion
Goldman Sachs Group Inc. $957.19 Billion

Morgan Stanley $865.52 Billion
US Bancorp $464.64 Billion
TD Group US Holdings LLC $380.65 Billion
PNC Financial Services $380.08 Billion
Capital One Financial Corp. $362.91 Billion

So let's explore the ways that the banks in the USA get bigger and richer every day.

You can ask all the citizens who have their savings in banks and they will tell you that the banks pay very low interest on their savings.

Now ask them what their banks charge them on their credit cards. We have savings accounts being paid one percent or less and credit cards being charged eighteen to twenty-one per cent.

With fees, banks have figured out how to charge you so that they can make extra money off your money. Check your next bank statement for all the fees you are being charged.

High Cost of a College Education

The cost of a college education is skyrocketing and this puts stress on the family.

The cost to attend a university has increased eight times faster than the increase in wages. Average parents cannot afford to send their children to college, so the children have to go to our wonderful banks and put their future in hock.

Too many of our universities are like our corporations: they want to grow larger and more powerful and do not have the interest of their clients (students) at heart.

I was shocked at the cost of our daughter's four years of college in a state University. When one looks up the costs, one rarely sees the total costs of keeping a child in college. It is not just the cost of tuition and books.

Deadbeat Parents

According to an article written by Brandon Gaille, May 24, 2017 only 72.9% of children are actually receiving the child support that they have been court-ordered to receive.

This lack of child support payment runs both ways, although men are the biggest non-payers. I, as a divorced father, paid my child support payments without fail and also kicked in a lot more for what my children needed. When I got my children from my wife, she never kicked in a dime.

I am a firm believer that if a man gets a woman pregnant that by law he should be required to help support that child. That should go both ways, a woman should by law be required to help support a father who is raising the child or children.

The most common reason why fathers decide not to pay child support is because they are denied any visitation rights. Over 90% of the fathers who are ordered to pay child support do so when they receive joint custody of their children.

Authority/Lack of Compromise

My mother and father were both alcoholics. They could not live with each other and they could not live without each other.

They were married to each other four times and divorced each other three times. The conflict between them was the reason my father was told he must retire and get out of the US Air Force.

My mother was a very strong woman and truly believed that she was smarter than my father and she should run things. My father did not go along with her thoughts. One can imagine how this went over with a man who was 6' 4" tall, weighed 240 pounds, loved to fight and had fought in two wars.

Neither one of them could share authority or compromise. This caused many mental and physical conflicts. The four children were caught in the middle. We were in constant fear of a fight breaking out. These constant conflicts caused domestic violence and abuse to the children.

PTSD

The American Psychiatric Association describes Post-traumatic stress disorder (PTSD) "as a psychiatric disorder that can occur in people who have experienced or witnessed a traumatic event such as a *natural disaster, a serious accident, a terrorist act, war/combat, rape or other violent personal assault*".

The American Psychiatric Association says the symptoms of PTSD fall into four categories:

1. **Intrusive thoughts** *such as repeated, involuntary memories, distressing dreams; or flashbacks of the traumatic event.*
2. **Avoiding reminders** *of the traumatic event may include avoiding people, places, activities, objects and situations that bring on distressing memories.*
3. **Negative thoughts and feelings** *may include ongoing and distorted beliefs about oneself or others (e.g., "I am bad", "No one can be trusted"); ongoing fear, horror, anger, guilt or shame; much less interest in activities previously enjoyed; or feeling detached or estranged from others.*
4. **Arousal and reactive symptoms** *may include being irritable and having angry outbursts; behaving*

> *recklessly or in a self-destructive way, being easily startled; or having problems concentrating or sleeping.*

My father fought in WWII and the Korean War and suffered from PTSD. Look at the above symptoms and they look like a lot of what is going on nowadays between men and women.

MEDIA/NEWSPAPERS

Oh, where to start and where to end? I have watched degrading TV Shows about men, I have read degrading articles about men, I have listened to degrading speeches about men and I have, and I have, and I have.

Most of this negative press and media about men are coming from the east or west coast very large liberal cities.

One wonders what is in the water in these areas. Big newspapers and media companies seem to get joy out of pushing anything negative between the sexes.

Locations of largest Newspapers

New York Times New York City
Washington Post Washington DC
USA Today McLean, Virginia
Houston Chronicle Houston, TX
Wall Street Journal New York City
Chicago Tribune Chicago, IL

Los Angeles Times Los Angeles, CA
New York Post New York City

Locations of largest News Agencies

Associated Press New York, City
United Press International Boca Raton, FL

Locations of largest TV networks

Fox News New York City
NBC New York City
ABC New York City
CBS New York City
CNN Atlanta, GA
MSNBC New York City

One can immediately see that most of our news comes from New York, NY. Here are some of my thoughts on New York, NY:

- The city that has no idea how the rest of the country lives or what is important to the rest of the country.
- The city that thinks and reacts completely different from most of the country, the part it often dismisses as "flyover country."
- The city that is so liberal that a lot of the conservatives hide that they are conservative.
- The city that is so arrogant they think the people in the rest of the country are a bunch of dummies.
- The city that is obsessed with LGBTQ community.
- The city, most of whose inhabitants think it is OK to abort 1,000,000 US babies a year and at the same time claim we need more workers so we should let 1,000,000+ illegal aliens into the country per year.

- A city that hires the same people with the same old ideas between the news agencies so that the public gets the same crap in their news year after year.

Let's play a little game. Let's try and get any article that says good things about men or women. I went to Google and asked the following:

A list of good things, men have done for women? (Below is a list of articles that came up)

- Men, you want to treat women better? Here's a list to start with
- 15 Things Women want from the Men in Their Lives
- 61 things Donald Trump has said about women
- 15 Things Men Say that Get on Women's Nerves
- 20 things Men Can do to Support Women
- 11 Women who did groundbreaking things that Men got the credit for
- Ten Things Men are good for
- Nine Things Women do that drive men away
- Ten Important Qualities of a Good Man

A list of good things women have done for men (Below is a list of articles that came up)

- 15 Things Women want from the Men in their lives
- Men, you want to treat women better? Here's a list

- 11 Women who did groundbreaking things that men got the credit for
- Important women through history
- 61 things Donald Trump has said about women
- The different words we use to describe Male and Female leaders
- Ten Things Women do that drive Men away
- Lust is complicated, but studies show these 19 things make men
- Ten Important Qualities of a Good Man

Does anyone see any article that is positive about men or women doing anything good for one another?

I tried different variations on the question and all I got was more of the same.

Does this mean that all we are being fed is negative crap on men and women or does it mean Google is negative about the sexes? Maybe both?

I have found that I have a better day when I do not watch TV News. I did away with the Fox News Channel because all it did was keep me upset.

That is what today's media tries to do, keep one upset.

Life is way too short to be upset all the time.

I read an article on Raptitude.com called "Five Things You Notice When You Quit the News" and it was so right on(44A). Here they are:

- *You feel better*
- *You were never actually accomplishing anything by watching the news.*

- *Most current-events-related conversations are just people talking out of their ass.*
- *There are much better ways to be "informed."*
- *"Being concerned" makes us feel like we're doing something when we're not.*

The nice thing about a newspaper, magazine or a book is one can throw it away if you don't like what they are writing. I am amazed by how fast my garbage can fills with propaganda.

DO WE CHOOSE LOVE?

Love is patient, love is kind, it does not boast, it is not proud. It is not rude, it s not self- seeking, it is not easily angered, it keeps no records of wrongs. Love does not delight in evil but rejoices with the truth. It always protects, always trusts, always hopes, always perseveres.
   1 *Corinthians* 13: 4-7

DO U.S. WOMEN REALLY HAVE IT SO BAD?

THERE ARE 195 COUNTRIES IN THE WORLD AND THE UNITED States ranks ninth for being the safest for women. I have to believe that this means something. Just think what women go through in the other 186.

According to an article by Olivia Ward(75), March 8, 2008, https://www.thestar.com these are the worst countries to live in if you are a woman:

- Afghanistan
- Democratic Republic of Congo
- Iraq
- Nepal
- Sudan
- Guatemala
- Mali
- Pakistan

- Saudi Arabia

Chris Pash's(58) article in the Business Insider Australia, January 23, 2018. "The 10 safest countries for women in 2017," shows the rankings based on the percentages of the female populations that have been victims of serious crimes over the past year (uk.businessinsider.com).

1. Australia
2. Malta
3. Iceland
4. New Zealand
5. Canada
6. Poland
7. Monaco
8. Israel
9. USA
10. South Korea

U.S. women well outlive U.S. men by a number of years (36).

U.S. women control 60% of the wealth in the US; the following came from a article written for "Women's History Month."(76)

- *The number of wealthy women in the U.S. is growing twice as fast as the number of wealthy men.*
- *Forty-five percent of American millionaires are women.*
- *Women control forty-eight percent of estates worth more than five million dollars.*
- *It is estimated that by 2030, women will control two-thirds of the nation's wealth.*

U.S. Women are Inheriting More. (10)

According to a 2009 study from the Boston College's Center on Wealth and Philanthropy, women will inherit 70% of the money that gets passed down over the next two generations—excluding the increasing amounts they earn on their own. Women already own more than half of the investable assets in the U.S..

U.S Women are earning more than ever. Here are the top-paid female CEOs May 26, 2018:

1. Indra Nooyi, PepsiCo, $25.9 million, Change from previous year: Up 3 percent
2. Debra Cafaro, Ventas, $25.3 million, Change from previous year: Up 161 percent
3. Mary Barra, General Motors, $21.9 million, Change from previous year: Down 2 percent
4. Phebe Novakovic, General Dynamics, $21.2 million, Change from previous year: Flat
5. Lynn Good, Duke Energy, $21.1 million, Change from previous: Up 57 percent
6. Marillyn Hewson, Lockheed Martin, $20.2 million, Change from previous year: Up 4 percent
7. Virginia Rometty, IBM, $18 million, Change from previous year: Down 44 percent
8. Margaret Whitman, Hewlett Packard Enterprise, $14.8 million, Change from previous year: Down 55 percent
9. Margaret Keane, Synchrony Financial, $13.5 million, Change from previous year: Up 32 percent
10. Heather Bresch, Mylan, $12.7 million, Change from previous year: Down 4 percent

---

U.S. Men do most of the dangerous work

. . .

Government data show that men suffer most of the workplace fatalities that take place in a given year.

In 2015, there were 4,836 workplace deaths, according to the Bureau of Labor Statistics. Of those, 4,492 were men, and 344 were women.

From 2011 through 2015, men accounted for 92.5% of all workplace deaths. It seems that men take most of the dangerous jobs (51).

Here are the 10 most dangerous jobs—think about when was the last time you saw a woman working at one of them:

1. *Logging workers*
2. *Fishers and fishing workers*
3. *Aircraft pilots and flight engineers*
4. *Roofers*
5. *Refuse and recyclable material collectors*
6. *Structural iron and street workers*
7. *Truck Drivers*
8. *Farmers, ranchers and agricultural managers*
9. *First line supervisors of construction trades and extraction workers*
10. *Grounds maintenance workers*

For many of the jobs cited above, women are just physically not as strong as men and therefore not seen in these jobs.

Then again, women may just be more clever than men in their commonsense avoidance of the most dangerous jobs.

U.S. Government spends most of the Health Care/Research dollars on women.

. . .

Why does the U.S. government spend more money on women's health when in fact it's men who die earlier?

This is a great question asked by Tom Luso(43) in an article dated November 8, 2015. He goes on to state:

> In the budget of every federal health agency, more money is spent on women's health than on men's. There are seven federal health agencies specifically for women. Not one for men.

However, although a woman is only 14 percent more likely to die from breast cancer than a man is from prostate cancer, funding for breast cancer research is 660% greater than funding for prostate cancer research. (43)

Is less spending on men's healthcare the cause of men's earlier mortality statistics?

Most U.S. men physically protect women against all dangers.

There is not a second in the day that I as a man do not have the protection of my wife and children on my mind.

My daughter, Kaylee, once asked me why I always walk in back of my family when we are out and about. That is because I want to be able to see what is coming at them from the front and sides and guard their back.

I have on two occasions scared off purse-snatchers with this tactic. I do not believe women realize the attention and energy that men put into protecting them continuously. (59)

Our eyes are always watching and our senses are always feeling the surroundings for dangers. Men have always put themselves in between danger and their loved ones. We do this instinctively. It is part of our makeup.

When my wife and I were newly married, my wife sometimes shouted at other drivers and made gestures at them. One day she did this and I asked her to pull out of the traffic and pull over. When she stopped the car I looked her in the eyes and asked her if she loved me. She said of course I love you, why did you ask that now? This is what I said: "If because of your actions, a car pulls us over and a bunch of mad guys get out, I am the one that is going to put myself between them and you. I will probably get hurt or killed. If you love me, do not put me in that situation".

A good example of this instinct of men to protect women is the article written by Nicole Darrah(10), September 12, 2018, for FoxNews.com. A woman ran into a Starbucks in Bakersfield screaming please help me.

There was a man chasing her with a machete in his hand. Blaine Hodge, a young man of 27, jumped between her and the assailant to protect her. He was stabbed many times and required 200 stitches. He may lose his right hand. He protected a woman that he did not know and saved her life.

Another example of the instinct of men to protect women is the incident in the Borderline Bar & Grill(2) in Thousand Oaks, California.

Eleven people were killed by a deranged shooter; during the time of the many shots being fired, a group of men got on their knees and turned their backs to the shooter to keep other people from being shot.

Other men broke windows and lifted women through the

windows to get them out of harm's way.

For the most part, the women these men were protecting were complete strangers.

U.S. Men do not require Women to help fight our wars as much as men do.

One million one hundred-thousand+ men have died, and three to five million have been maimed or crippled in all the wars that the United States has fought since becoming a Republic.

After hours of research on the number of women who fought and died in these same wars, the best figure I could come up with was about twenty thousand.

Now let's do some math.

Divide 20,000 by 1,100,000 and one gets one point eight (1.8) percent of the deaths in all our wars were women.

That tends to lead me to the belief that not many women fought in our wars.

The government drafted the majority of these men who died, were maimed or disabled. They could not say **my body, my choice.**

U.S. women won the vote August 26, 1920 with the passage of the 19th Amendment, yet they do not have to register for the draft.

Some say that doesn't matter because the U.S. hasn't drafted anyone for over forty years.

Yes, but the Selective Service System remains in place as a contingency plan: all male civilians between the ages of 18 and 25 are required to register so that a draft can be readily resumed if needed.

Even non-citizens and dual nationals are required by law to register with the Selective Service System.

In other words, in a matter of days the government could restart the draft.

If you are required to register and you don't, you will not be eligible for federal student aid, federal job training, a federal job, or U.S. citizenship. You may be prosecuted and face a stiff fine and/or jail time.

Failing to register or comply with the Military Selective Service Act is a felony punishable by a fine up to $250,000 or a prison term of up to five years, or a combination of both.

Representative Duncan Hunter introduced an amendment to expand the draft to women in April 2016 and it passed 32-30 in the House Armed Services Committee but the provision was taken out of the final House bill.

The amendment was passed in the Senate also but was stripped out of the final Senate bill.

The final law that was passed was to establish a commission to study the draft's future use.

The feminist movement will tell you that we have a lot of women serving in our military and they are right.

I salute these women as one veteran to another and I thank them for their service.

According to a Pew Research Center article dated April 13, 2017 the Department of Defense said that overall, 15% of our active duty military personnel are women, 51% of the USA population are women. (77)

. . .

U.S. Men are still paying most of the costs when dating.

The American Sociological Association found that 84% of men and 58% of women say that men should pay for most entertainment expenses (60). Most men believe women should contribute at some point to dating expenses.

The writer Gerda(35) wrote an article called *Guy refuses to pay $126 for his date's food, so she shows him her true colors* which relates to how some women abuse men on dates. It seems this woman asked this young man out on a first date. His food cost $17.50 (a Carbonara and a beer) and hers (Lobster and $80.00 wine) cost $110.00, totaling with tax $127.50. When he only paid for his part of the meal, she was not pleased and her statement was "Gentlemen ALWAYS pay for girl's food but I guess you are gay." What does being gay have to do with sharing the costs of a meal?

WHAT DO MEN AND WOMEN LOOK FOR WHEN DATING?

Anthony D'Ambrosio(82) wrote an article in May of 2015, in the Elite Daily, that I find very interesting. The article is titled: **What men want: 7 traits men look for in the lady of their dreams.** What is really amazing to me is I believe that these same seven traits are what women are looking for in a man when they are dating:

1. Character
2. Respect
3. Affection
4. Intelligence
5. Confidence
6. Ambition
7. Humility

Notice none of these qualities have anything to do with looks or parts of the body.

Mr. D'Ambrosio writes in his article that men are really turned on sexually by the above. Wow! I believe women are also turned on sexually by the above. Good looks are just a plus.

Suzanne Venker wrote an article for FOX NEWS, May 2017, that I think hit it right on the head on what men are looking for,

---

"Most men just want a woman who's nice." (74B)

Her definition of nice is doing something for someone without expectation of getting something in return.

In other words, you think of others before you think of yourself.

In this article, Ms. Venker made a statement that I think is priceless. More women need to learn this—

"most husbands have no desire to lord over their wives, but they don't want to fight with them either. All they want is peace."

So why do men make so many mistakes when they are interacting with women trying to get a date or when dating.

Well ladies, young men really do not have a clue about how to converse with you or what you are all about. We stumble through the process doing the best we can with what we have to work with.

I will bet money that most young girls and women are in the same boat when it comes to boys and men.

We spend twelve years in school and if we are lucky four years in college being taught all kinds of things, except the most important, how to converse and act with the opposite sex.

We work in industry and they do not hold classes on how men and women must converse and interact. Oh, I know that one can find a course in some colleges on how women are being taken advantage of and how they should protect themselves. I also know that almost every employer is holding training sessions on sexual harassment and how men are usually the problem.

WHAT IS LOVE ABOUT?

The *Good Men Project* had a great article January 16, 2017 written by James Michael Sama, "***7 Signs of true love from a man***." You women who have a man who loves you to infinity will recognize these signs.

1. *He includes you in every part of his life.*
2. *He tries to give more than he takes.*
3. *It's not "**me**," it's "**us**."*
4. *He really sees you.*
5. *Your happiness is his happiness.*
6. *He's there for you even on the rainy days.*
7. *You will know.*

John Cyril Abello wrote an article, "***12 Real Signs of True Love from a Woman***"(10a) that is right on in the signs that a woman loves you.

1. *She takes care of you like a mom.*
2. *She is willing to sacrifice for you.*

3. *She is kind and patient no matter how annoying you are.*
4. *She forgives you many times.*
5. *She does not tolerate the bad things you do.*
6. *She pushes you to be a better person.*
7. *She encourages and supports you in reaching your dreams.*
8. *She stays with you in your darkest times.*
9. *She introduces you to her family and friends.*
10. *She does things to get closer to your loved ones.*
11. *She will not take advantage of you.*
12. *She does not take you for granted.*

I know when I was dating as a young man, I had no idea what I was looking for in the person I was dating nor did I have a clue of what love was about.

A LOVE STORY

The love between a woman and a man is truly the greatest gift that God has ever given us. Love gives our lives so much meaning. Love helps us grow, learn and understand what we are created for. Love helps us understand and forgive our partner's mistakes in life. Love gives us a safe haven from all the bad things that life throws our way. Love gives us children, who bring us so much joy. Love keeps a smile on our face.

I FEEL THAT IT IS IMPORTANT TO TELL YOU THIS LOVE STORY. We all need to understand why men and women date. It is not because we are so much alike that we have to be together.

Quite the opposite, we are so different that it is amazing that we get together at all. The dating dance is to see if the couple is compatible enough to stay together over a long period of time so that a family can be raised.

. . .

Here is my love story.

I was age 33, had been divorced for a while, and I was teaching classes at a Junior College once a week.

Usually I would go to the student center before class to go over my class notes. On one of these class days I was coming through the front door of the student center and almost ran into a young lady of 23.

I was immediately attracted to her. She had a smile and a twinkle in her eyes that was very alluring, and with the few words she used to say she was sorry, she caught my attention.

The next week's class day I am sitting in the student center going over my class notes when this same young lady approaches me. She said, "Hi, I am Jan and I am going to Dental Hygiene School. How would you like to get your teeth X-rayed, free? She smiled that beautiful smile and the twinkle in her eyes was mesmerizing, and I replied, "That is quite a line, do you mind if I use it?"

That short conversation turned out to be a loving relationship for over 43 years and still going strong. I believe that God has one great love for all of us. We just need to date to find that one person.

I was raised in a dysfunctional family where the parents were alcoholics and were abusive to each other and their children.

There was no love in the family and so the children had no example of what love was or how it should look. Four abused boys had to go out into the world and find love. One can imagine what their lives looked like and the roads they had to travel.

I feel very sorry for my first wife. I was totally unprepared to be a husband or a father and the marriage failed mainly due to my ignorance.

God gave me a second chance and sent a woman to me who was the perfect match of what I needed in my troubled life.

This woman helped me raise three boys by my previous marriage and a girl we had together. The two of us sent all four children to college, which we paid for so that the children did not start out their lives in debt.

The children all turned out to be great adults and we now have six grandchildren. Was it all wine and roses? No. Lots of love and forgiveness along the way indeed.

During this love affair we traveled all over the world and the United States together. We tried to do everything together that both of us wanted to do:

1. made 50 scuba dives together
2. took sailing lessons to learn to sail
3. took flying lessons
4. went to *Chapman's Professional Mariners School In order to obtain our "100 Ton Masters License" to captain ships*
5. *bare-boated a 42' Beneteau sailboat around the Virgin Islands for 10 days*
6. *sailed and yachted the San Juan Islands*
7. *played cowboys on two ranches we owned*
8. *lived full time in a 40' Winnebago traveling all over the United States for a year*
9. *still own an RV and travel the US periodically*
10. *made numerous ocean and river cruises*
11. *played tennis and golf together*

During this same 43 years, we lived through Jan having cervical cancer, me having nine stents put in my heart. We both worked full time during this period, sharing the economic responsibility of raising a family and we shared taking care of what needed to be done in the house/yard we lived in.

The point I am trying to make is that we shared everything, the good, bad and the ugly. We made a lot of mistakes, especially me.

My mother physically, mentally and verbally abused her husband and all her children. One can only imagine what my impression of women was, but Jan and I were committed to each other and Jan was very forgiving of all my faults and mistakes and her kindness and love helped me heal from my childhood.

Today my wife and I celebrated our 40th wedding anniversary and this is what her card to me said:

You are the quiet strength I lean on, the steady presence I count on for so much. Thank you for being there whatever life brings us, and loving me even on the days when I get busy and forget how much that means. You're a good man, and the longer we're married the better I know it. I love you Sam. OXOXOX

These words made me feel like I just received the **Medal of Honor of LIFE** because she knows how much I love her. If you want the whole love story, check out my book, "When Love Doesn't Start at Home."

The reason I put this love story here is to remind everybody why we date. We date to find love. We do not date to get ahead in our job, to get a part in a movie, to have a good time at the other participant's expense or to show off to everyone who we are with. When we forget the true reason for dating, is when we end up having problems.

HOW CAN WE CHANGE?

RELATIONSHIP/FAMILY TRAINING

In my working years in the financial world, 42 of them, I had to continuously train and retrain myself. By that, I mean that I was required to take continuing education classes for all the licenses and professional certifications I held. This amounted to about thirty hours a year spent training and retraining myself.

Think about it, one cannot get a driver's license without training in books and a driving test. Most professions require extensive training to get a license and continuous retraining to keep it.

In other words, one cannot work at almost anything without training and retraining every year.

Now let's think about the most important things that we do in life —relationships, marriage and raising children. How much formal training did you get in how to start and maintain relationships? How much formal training did you get about love and marriage? How much formal training did you get on raising children?

We spend twelve years in school to learn reading, writing and arithmetic. We spend another four years in college to get a degree in our interest of life, another two years to get our Master's Degree and maybe more years for additional degrees. Then most of us spend the rest of our lives trying to keep up with work by additional training.

I believe that those first sixteen years of schooling should have mandatory classes in relationships, love, how to communicate and how a family lives and functions. Every grade from pre-school through college should have at least an hour a day on these subjects.

The PAIRS Foundation did a Relationship Education Impact Study for the US Department of Health and Human Services. Here are a few of the headlines on what was learned (57A):

- *Lasting Impact of Marriage Education*
- *Marriage and Relationship Education Benefits Singles Too*
- *Positive Enduring, Impact for Low-Income Participants*
- *Relationship Skills Training Reduces Marital Breakdown*
- *Study Shows More Women Satisfied with Sex Lives After Marriage Classes*
- *Men Increasingly Investing in Marriage/Relationship Education*
- *Relationship Skills Training Could Prevent Four out of Five Divorces*

Jill Ceder wrote an excellent article, "Should I Take a Parenting Class?"

"The purpose of parenting classes is to help parents feel more connected, involved and focused on their children. Parenting classes provide advice, strategies, and tools on how to raise children and provide an opportunity for parents to share ideas and concerns with parents going through similar issues. These classes educate parents on how to take care of their babies, toddlers, and teens. Parents come away from classes feeling more confident about and more supported in their parenting decisions."

These parenting classes should be ongoing for as long as there are children in the home.

Also in these classes there should be training on what happens in life financially. This should start out with this is a penny, a nickel and so on.

Daniel Thompson on Feb. 8, 2018 wrote an article for the Council for Economic Education, "*2018 Survey of the States Reveals Slow to No Growth in K-12. Personal Finance and Economic Education*". (72B) It details that K-12 students are not receiving adequate tools and training to make informed financial decisions.

BRING BACK THE DRAFT

When I was young and dropped out of high school, I had no idea what I was going to do and I did not have a clue on what life was about and how I should live it.

The US had a draft then. I joined the US Navy. I was just a punk kid of seventeen and dumb as hell. Eight years in the military taught me so many things:

- *How to be a man*
- *The value of an education*
- *How lucky I was to be an American*
- *Discipline*
- *Sacrifice*
- *The gratification of hard work*
- *Cooperation*
- *Goal Setting*

I believe our younger generation needs some training in all the above.

Also our younger generation needs to be educated.

This is my proposal: Have a draft for two years for all young people, men and women. One could either serve in the military or in something like the Peace Corps. For that service, the US Government would pay for the first two years of college when their two years of service is completed.

I believe not only would it be a great benefit to our young people, I guarantee it would cut the whining factor by 80%, and it would contribute to a happier, healthier country at large.

PRESS/MEDIA

Have you ever read an article or watched a TV news program and wonder what is this all about?

Have you ever read an article or watched a TV news program and felt your blood pressure rising?

Have you ever watched a TV news program and started shouting at the TV. Have you ever watched a TV news program and felt very depressed afterwards?

Guess what—this is their intent, to get you so upset that you remember them.

I was born in 1942, and started watching the news on TV when I was about thirteen.

From 1955 up through the 1980's, TV news programs pretty much gave one the straight news. You could almost bet that what they were saying was pretty close to the truth. (Where is a Walter Cronkite now when we really need him?)

Now I do not watch TV news programs. In my opinion they are pretty much crap. They are geared to keep a person upset about something. One almost never sees a story about anything that happens that is good. The fact checking before they air, is pretty much non-existent. Most of the news is coming from the east or west coast very liberal large cities. It is like the source does not know that there are people who live in the heartland.

In my opinion, they hire commentators and journalist who hate something or someone and everything they say or write one can see the hate oozing out.

I do not get the feeling that one can trust any of these news sources. I don't believe they are giving us the straight news but what they want us to believe. FAIR wrote an article called, **What's Wrong with the News?** I am going to give you a few quotes from that article:

> "Profit-driven news organizations are under great pressure to boost ratings by sensationalizing the news: focusing attention on lurid emotional stories, often featuring a bizarre cast of characters and a gripping plot but devoid of significance to most peoples' lives".

I believe this is what is being played with our relationship between men, women and families.

Hate sells.

It is very dangerous. According to FAIR, pressure groups have a lot to do with what we see and read. Here is what FAIR says is the role of a pressure group:

> "a pressure group is more concerned with suppressing viewpoints that it disagrees with than ensuring that a wide range of perspectives is available."

Another important quote from FAIR's article:

"Independent, aggressive and critical media are essential to an informed democracy. But mainstream media are increasingly cozy with the economic and political powers they should be watchdogging."

How do we fix it? I believe that these large news organizations need to be broken up much like the government broke up AT&T.

We have too much news coming from too few organizations. The fact checking needs to be done before it goes to print or shows on TV. We need at least two good sources to verify the story. If the outlet cannot disclose the name of the source, the story shouldn't be printed or seen. Yes, I know I am not a lawyer but a little common sense should be used.

WHAT CAN WOMEN AND MEN DO?

Go Abroad
I do not believe women and men that live in the USA realize just how good their lives are compared to the rest of the world.

Please travel, and pay attention to the lives of women and men in other countries.

I am not talking about going to Europe, I am talking about visiting the other 80% of the world that is not in the Western Civilization.

Pay Attention to Your Partner
Stop listening so much to your friends, mothers, sisters, fathers and brothers and start listening more to the one who loves you. Theirs is the opinion that should carry most of the weight.

Speak up for the opposite sex
Not everything that goes wrong in the world is the fault of the opposite sex. When someone starts to complain and you know it is a

false complaint, say something. Keep in mind that all this false negativity is going to affect the person in your life that you care about.

Read more about the other sex

Just as men are ignorant about women and their feelings and needs, so are women ignorant about a man's feelings and needs. Let's all of us spend more time learning about each other.

Teachers

Boys and girls are different and they learn and perceive differently. Please stop thinking that we should act and learn the same way.

Avoid confrontation

Just because the other sex does not say anything does not mean that they agree with you. Men shy away from confrontation because they have learned at a young age that confrontation could get them hurt. Start asking each other how the other feels.

Write and Boycott

Start writing letters and boycotting the establishments that you know are anti-male or anti-female. Loss of profits does get attention.

Question

What is good for the gander is also good for the goose. When one sex does something, look at it as if the other sex were doing it. Would the other sex be called racist or sexist? Would they go to jail for it?

A women's bathroom is filled to capacity so a woman walks into a man's bathroom being used by men and takes a booth. If a man were to do this in a women's bathroom, the law would likely be called and he might be charged.

Remember a while back when female news reporters complained that they could not get the same breaks as males reporting sports events because they couldn't go into the men's locker rooms? So, guess what, female reporters were allowed to go into the men's locker rooms while they were showering and getting dressed. Did you see the opposite happen with female locker rooms?

Be proud of both Sexes

God made us all with our own talents. None of us are better than the other.

Get involved

Get into some activity whose objective is to level the playing field between the sexes.

Speak your mind

When some woman or man makes an uninformed statement or remark about the opposite sex, correct them but be kind.

Control your sexual urges

Sex is wonderful, but it can get us into a lot of trouble.

Watch how you dress

Sexual harassment goes both ways.

Point out discrimination

Every time you see discrimination against a male or female, no matter large or small, point it out and fight it. (73)

Fight false accusations

Do not take gossip to be the truth. If an accusation cannot be proven with facts, it is not real. If the accusation is false, the accuser should suffer the same fate as the accused would have suffered.

Make laws fair to all

What is good for the Gander is good for the Goose. Once a reputation is lost it is hard to retrieve. If it is unfair to reveal the females name in sexual cases, it is also unfair to reveal the male's name until proven guilty.

Be completely humble and gentle; be patient, bearing with one another in love.

1 CORINTHIANS 16:14

REFERENCES/BACKGROUND RESOURCES

REFERENCE #) AUTHOR, ARTICLE ENTITY

(1) AP, "Woman accused of lying about Fox News being raped offered plea deal"

(1a) John Abello, "12 Real Signs of True Love from a Woman"

(1b) Barrons, "Americans don't save for retirement because they don't earn enough"

(2) Hank Berrien, "Real Men: Witness says men in Daily Wire Thousand Oaks shooting knelt to block shooter from shooting others"

(3) James Barrett, 'Woman arrested after posting video CBS of herself raping 5-year-old boy"

(4) Tammy Bruce, "The Democrats "believe all women Fox News fraud"

86　SAMMY GOTT

(4a) Sherrie Campbell, "The four benefits of conflict" Entrepeneur

(4b) Jill Cedar, "Should I take a parenting class"

(5) Samuel Chamberlain "Weinstein accuser Asia Argento Fox News made deal to pay her own sexual accuser, bombshell report says"

(6) Christina Cauterucci, "Why the feud between Asia Relationships Argento and Rose McGowan Is so incredibly dispiriting"

(7) Dom Calicchio, "Male student molested by Fox News female teacher awarded 2.1M"

(8) V Wigglesworth, "Ex-Plano teacher who sent Dallas Morning News nude pics, played beer pong with student gets probation for improper relationship"

(9) Nicole Darrah, "Bella Thorne wants out of Fox News #MeToo movement after new Asia Argento claims"

(10) Nicole Darrah, "Calif. Man steps in front of Fox News machete to save woman at, Starbucks"

(11) Caroline Davis, "Harvey Weinstein: the women The Guardian who have accused him"

(12) Jack Davis, "Abortion Tops 2018 list of all US News causes of Death, Over 41M Worldwide"

(13) Paulina Dedaj, "Former Miss Kentucky charged Fox News with sending obscene" photos to student"

(14) Edmund DeMarche , "University of Minnesota change Fox

News scholarship rule after anti-male discrimination allegation: report"

(15) Edmund DeMarche, "Dine-and-dash dater faces 10 Fox News felony counts for allegedly skipping out on dates before bill"

(16) Rod Dreher, "Manhood as Mental Disorder" American Conservative

(17) Breck Dumas, "Gender inequality? Global The BLAZE study finds men face more discrimination than women"

(18) Jennifer Earl, "Kentucky radio station plays Fox New "Baby, its Cold Outside" on repeat amid backlash"

(19) Sara R Edwards, "Would a third of male students Guerrilla Ontology commit rape – Methodological flaws in new study"

(20) Sara R Edwards, "Denying rape but endorsing Kathryn Bradshaw Violence & forceful intercourse: Verlin b Hinsz Exploring differences among Gender responders", Asia Argento's accuser Jimmy

(21) Entertainment & Arts Bennet speaks out"

(22) Entrepreneur.com, "Will decriminalization of Sex Fox News Work become the next anti-Regulation battle?"

(22A) FAIR, "What's Wrong with the News?"

(23) Warren Farrell, "Why are so many Campus Minding The Campus Feminists Anti-Male?"

(24) Laura Fitzpatrick, "Female primary school teacher
The Telegraph sexually assaulted male colleague at parent's evening"

(25) Brian Flood, "Asia Argento denies sex assault Fox News allegations, says Anthony Bourdain paid accuser"

(26) Quentin Fottrell, "I paid for my girlfriend's rent, marketwatch.com. food, vacations and utilities while she was in college—now we are breaking up"

(27) David French, "Here's one thing Tucker Carlson
The Corner gets really right"

(28) "Substitute teacher, 23, accused Fox News of having sex with two students, including 14-year-old"

(29) "Teen's dad busted Texas teacher, Fox News 44, having sex with student in car, police say"

(30) "Special ed teacher, mother of 5 Fox News gets 10 years for sex with teen boy student"

(31) "Married English teacher, 32, Fox News pleads not guilty to charge of booze-filled sex with teen boy student"

(32) Michelle Gant, "Angry bride releases 10-year-old
Fox News letter to sister who stole her spot light before wedding: Thank you for all your thoughtlessness"

(33) Michelle Gant, "Bridezilla's demanding list of Fox News wedding dress code requirements goes viral: If you look trash, so will we"

33a) Brandon Gaille, "25 Important Deadbeat Dad Statistics

(34) Ryan Gaydos, "Drake reportedly claims in lawsuit Fox News woman attempted to extort him using false rape, pregnancy claims"

(35) Gerda, "Guy refuses to pay $126 for his date's Bored Panda food, so she shows him her true colors"

(35a) Joshua Gowin, "Under Pressure: Your brain on conflict" Psychology Today

(36) SS Admin, "Probability of a 65-year-old living Hamilton Brookings to a given age, by Sex and Year"

(36a) C. Hayes, "I was angry and I sent it" USA Today

(37) M. Hendrickson, "Chicago Public Schools teaching Chicago Teaching assistant accused of sexually assaulting young student"

(38) The National, "Get the facts & figures on rape" Domestic Violence Hotline

(38a) Catherine Huang, "8 Common Characteristics of a Dysfunctional Family"

(39) Charles Hymas, "Growing number of Men reporting Home Affairs domestic violence to police" Patrick Scott

(40) Kathleen Joyce, "Serial 'dine-and-dash dater' Fox News sentenced to jail and prohibited from using dating apps"

(41) Sarah Knapton, "Strangers scared to give female The Telegraph heart attack victims CPR in case they're accused of sexual assault"

42 Howard Kurtz, "NY Times uncovers troubling

Fox News questions about its reporter's affair with Senate official

(42a) LifeSet, "Young Men Giving up on Marriage"

(43) Tom Luso, "Why does the US Government spend more money on women's health when in fact it's men who die earlier?"

(44) Richard Madely, "Dear Richard" The Telegraph

(44a) Raptitude, "Five things you notice when you quit the news"

(45) Kristine Mae, "Moms are tired of Superheroes Scarey Mommy who need help"

(46) Tyler McCarthy, "James Woods threatened over Fox News "#MeToo Issues" by Stormy Daniels lawyer Michael Avenatti"

(47) Tyler McCarthy, "Pamela Anderson blasts the #MeToo Fox News movement, says feminism can go too far"

(48) Tyler McCarthy, "CNN pulls Asia Argento"s episodes Fox News of Anthony Bourdain's 'Parts Unknown'"

(49) Martha McCallum, "HuffPost claims Sen. Collins' Fox News Kavanaugh support was "Shameful Hijacking of Feminism"

(50) J McDermott, "Lawsuit: Schools don't prepare AP kids for Civic Life"

(51) John Merline, "Gender Pay Gap? What about the Investors Business Daily workplace Death Gap?"

(52) #MeToo, "Statistics on Masculinity https://metoomvmt.com attitudes/Male attitudes"

(53) Rachel Morgan, "Criminal Victimization, 2016 US Dept. of Justice Revised" Grace Kena

(54) NY Post, "Asia Argento reportedly won't Fox News pay sexual assault accuser the rest of $380G"

(55) NY Post, "Woman finds her diamond Fox News before proposal and 'ring shames' herself"

(56) Greg Norman, "Fox Nations' Scandalous: The Fox News Mysterious Case of Tawana Brawley goes in-depth on the Lie that made Al Sharpton Famous"

(57) R Miller, "Teacher who had sex with student NY Post should get off easy because he wanted it: Lawyers"

(57a) Pairs Foundation, "Current Research on Marriage Relationship Education"

(58) Chris Pash, "The 10 safest countries in the Business Insider world for women Australia

(58a) Dennis Prager, "Are Women Malcontents" TownHall

(58b) Pew Research Center, "Social & Demographic Trends

(59) C Pumphrey, "Everything you need to know Meetmindful about the Male Mind"

(60) C Pearson, "Men still paying for dates and Huffington Post women are partly responsible"

(60a) Eric Reed, "How much do UBER & LYFT

The Street Vidio Drivers make in 2018"

(61) C Ritschel, "Is this the future of consensual sex?"

(62) E Romano, Why you should stay single,
Playbook for the according to a lot of research
Modern Man over 15 years"

(63) Jackie Salo, "Teacher called 'Kim Kardashian' Duluth News Tribune by students pleads guilty to sex acts with boys"

(63a) James Sama, "7 Signs of True Love from a man
The Good Men Project

(64) Ashe Schow, "She claimed a Police Officer Daily Wire raped her. Surveillance Footage determined that was a lie"

(65) Ashe Schow, "A Clemson student has been Fox News arrested after deputies say she falsely accused a man of raping her at a fraternity house party"

(66) Ashe Schow, "School pays male student $47k
The Ben Shapiro Show after it punished him based on nothing more than an accusation"

(67) Ashe Schow, "Mizzou official claims tall men Daily Wire asking out short women could constitute sexual misconduct"

(67a) Joanna Smykowski, "An Overview of Misoqyny"
Better Health

(68) J. Stossel, "Let's legalize prostitution. It's Fox News time for government to step away from sex work"

(69) Mary Sue, "Woman realizes that she's Heartwarming been accidentally abusing husband this whole time...

(70) Gillian Tan, "Wall Street Rule for the Bloomberg Business #MeToo era: Avoid women K. Porzecanski at all costs"

(70a) Anthony Skynnott, "Why Some People Have issues Re-thinking Man with Man"

(71) Jessica Tariov, "Good news—Kavanaugh vote Fox News delay proves that we are finally listening to women"

(72) Taboola, "Women are Inheriting More" AP

(72a) The Big Answer, "Family Dkysfunction"

(72b) Daniel Thompson, "2018 Survey of the States"

(73) J K Trotter, "The Wing quietly dropped its Inc. "No Men Allowed" practice after being sued for $12M in a discrimination lawsuit"

(74) C Turner, "Female primary school head The Telegraph admits child sex offenses as outraged parents thought she was off sick"

(74a) Suzanne Venker, "Is Equality Ruining Your Marriage" Fox News

(74b) Suzanne Venker, "Most Men Just want a Woman Fox News who is Nice"

(75) Olivia Ward, "Ten worst countries for women" The Star

(76) Women's History Month, "Women control the Wealth"

(77) M Wente, "Ladies, check your privilege" The Globe

(78) Wikipedia, "MeToo Movement" Wikipedia

(78a) Skheila Weber, "Marriage is a Great Anti-Poverty Fox News program"

(79) C Young, "CDC Rape numbers are Reason Magazine misleading"

(80) Z Zaczek, "Female staff member admits Daily Mail to having sex with five male teenage students at a prestigious school – but says she only did it because she was blackmailed"

(81) M C Cook, "Boys left to fail" The Telegraph

(82) A D'Ambrosio, "What men want. Elite Daily Traits men look for"

(83) S Venker, "The War on Men"

ALSO BY SAMMY GOTT

"When Love Doesn't Start At Home: Surviving a Dysfunctional Family"

It was hard being one of four boys growing up in the 1940s in a dysfunctional family. Throw in alcoholic parents, a hot tempered pure-bred American Indian mother, a father running secret missions for the military, and three wild brothers and you got a mix of family craziness.

This is a beautiful and engaging book about surviving and prospering after growing up in a dysfunctional family. It is told by a man who is a brother, husband, father, veteran, and overall good guy who has a lot of life lessons to share with the world.

For more information, visit http://www.sammyleegott.com/WLDSAH-info

---

"Life is a Series of Jokes"

This is a story of all the things that happen to a man from pre-birth to age 75 This book covers the events that a man has no control over but which affects his life and what direction his life goes. These twists and turns in life are very humorous and are accentuated by hundreds of jokes that fit the situations.

Sammy Lee Gott has been a son, brother, husband, father, soldier, and all around good guy for the last 75 years. During his life's journey, he has learned the power of humor. This is a collection of his personal story and plenty of jokes he's discovered.

For more information, visit http://sammyleegott.com/LIASOJ-info

---

"Neither Man Nor Woman is Spelled S.A.I.N.T."

We are in the crossroad of hate and love between men and women in the United States and right now hate is winning. This book explores some of the ways that we as a nation can be more on the side of love first by defining what love is and suggestions on how men and women can make a difference in this battle.

For more information, visit http://sammyleegott.com/NMNWISS-info

www.ingramcontent.com/pod-product-compliance
Lightning Source LLC
Chambersburg PA
CBHW022117090426
42743CB00008B/885